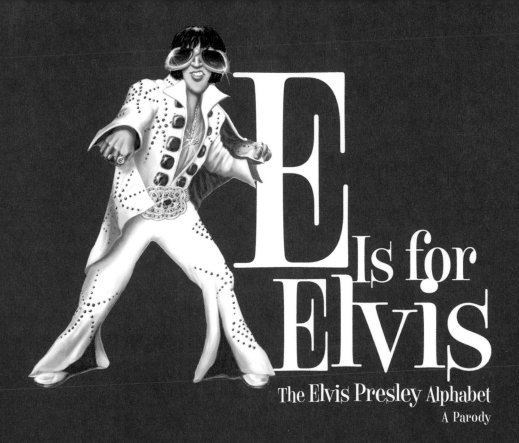

E Is for Elvis

The Elvis Presley Alphabet
A Parody

Jennie Ivey • W. Calvin Dickinson • Lisa W. Rand
Illustrated by Ron Wireman Jr.

RUTLEDGE HILL PRESS®
Nashville, Tennessee

A Division of Thomas Nelson Publishers
www.ThomasNelson.com

Published by Rutledge Hill Press, a Division of Thomas Nelson, Inc.,
P.O. Box 141000, Nashville, Tennessee 37214.

Rutledge Hill Press books may be purchased in bulk for educational, business, fundraising, or sales promotional use. For information, please e-mail SpecialMarkets@ThomasNelson.com.

Library of Congress Cataloging-in-Publication Data

Ivey, Jennie, 1954–
  E is for Elvis / Jennie Ivey, W. Calvin Dickinson, Lisa W. Rand ;
illustrated by Ron Wireman, Jr.
    p. cm.
  ISBN 1-4016-0240-1 (hardcover)
  1. Presley, Elvis, 1935–1977—Humor. I. Dickinson, W. Calvin. II. Rand, Lisa W., 1966– III. Wireman, Ron. IV. Title.
  ML420.P96I84 2006
  782.42166092—dc22   2005033777

Printed in the United States of America
06 07 08 09 10 — 5 4 3 2 1

To my late parents, Rayburn and Josephine Moore, who would be thrilled that their daughter has written a book. Especially one about Elvis.

—J. I.

To all the teens in the 1950s who loved or hated Elvis.

—W. C. D.

To some original Elvis fans: Mom and Dad, Aunt Lucille and Uncle Billy, and Aunt Loraine and my late Uncle Elwood.

—L. W. R

To my parents, who have always supported me, and to my wife, April, for her unending encouragement.

—R. W.

 # A Is for All Shook Up

Before Elvis, there was nothing.

—John Lennon

On the evening of July 7, 1954, Memphis disc jockey Dewey Phillips played a record called "That's All Right" by an unknown nineteen-year-old singer named Elvis Presley.

The phones at radio station **WHBQ** began ringing. Listeners didn't know—or care—if the singer was black or white. They weren't sure what kind of music he was performing. They just knew that they liked what they'd heard.

When Elvis Presley burst onto the scene, rock and roll was born. Rock and roll wasn't just about music, though. It was about clothes. It was about hairstyles. It was about a different way of thinking, moving, and behaving. And those new ways caused America, and much of the rest of the world, to forever become all shook up.

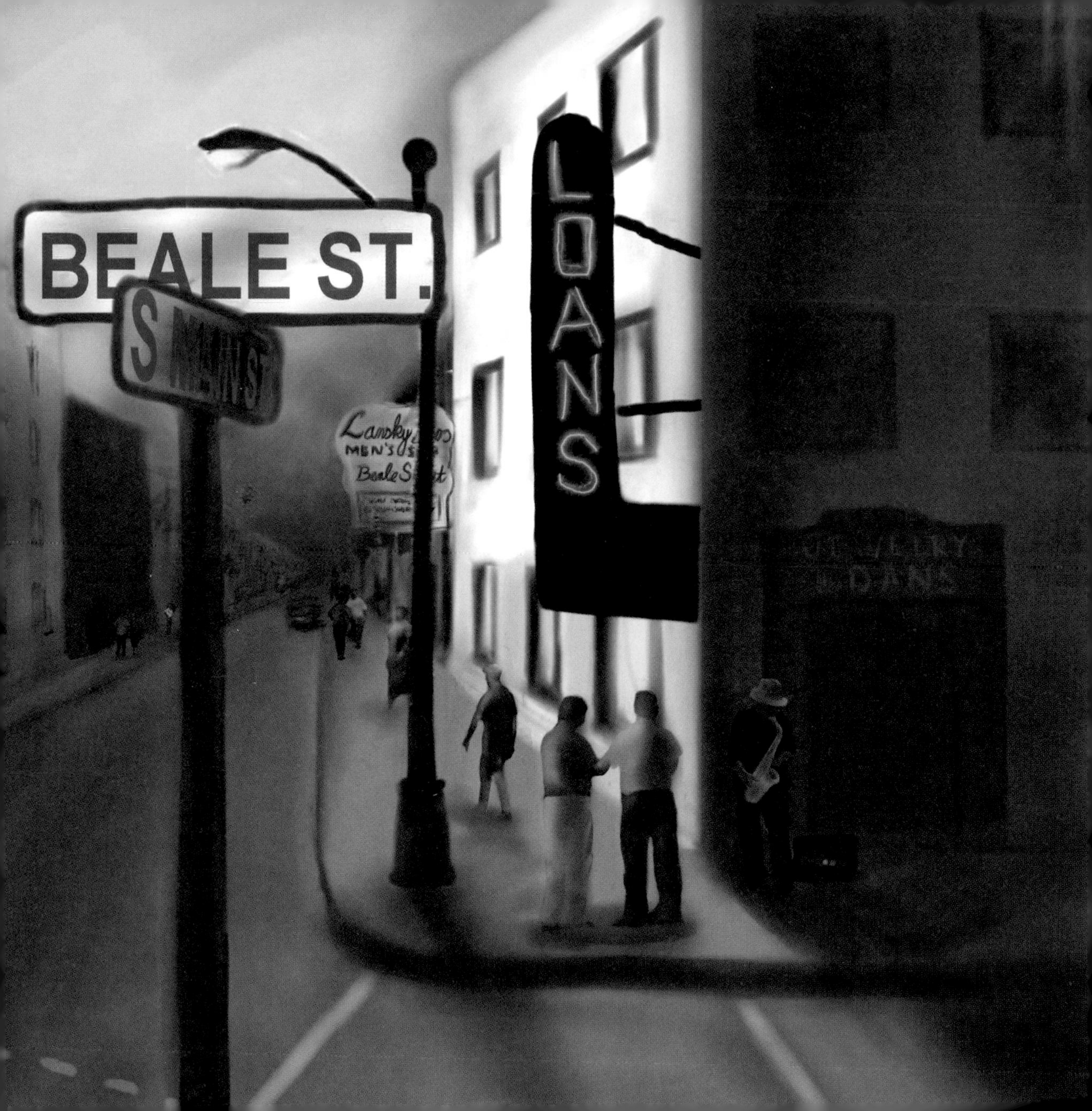
BEALE ST.
LOANS

B Is for Beale Street

People ask me why Elvis sounded black. I tell 'em how he would listen to WDIA, which was the first black radio station. And who knows what he heard down on Beale Street?

—Billy Smith, Elvis's cousin

Beale Street was Elvis's favorite Memphis hangout when he was in high school. In the lively black neighborhood where the blues had been invented, he spent hours on end listening to and learning to imitate black musicians.

Elvis's favorite store, Lansky Brothers Clothiers, was on Beale Street. He would press his face to their picture window and dream of the day when he might be able to afford the flashy outfits featured there.

Elvis recorded his first hit songs at Sun Studios near Beale Street. Sam Phillips, the white man who owned Sun, operated his business so that black musicians could have a place in Memphis to record their music.

C Is for "Colonel" Tom Parker

If Colonel Parker made Elvis Presley, then why didn't he make another one?
—Ricky Stanley, Elvis's stepbrother

"Colonel" Tom Parker wasn't really a colonel; he was an illegal immigrant who first made his living as a carnival worker and a dogcatcher. Then he became a talent agent for country singers.

The first time Parker saw Elvis perform, he knew the young singer was his ticket to wealth. Parker became Elvis's manager and persuaded him to leave Sun Records and sign with RCA.

Parker spent the next twenty years managing Elvis's career. Thanks in part to his efforts, Elvis became one of the biggest superstars in history. But many people believe that Parker put his own desire for fame and money above concerns about Elvis's well-being. Some critics even claim that Parker was partially to blame for Elvis's unhappiness and early death.

D Is for Death Day

When visiting Elvis's grave you should arrive before 7:30 a.m. to
avoid long lines. Also, never go on the anniversary of his death
or you will encounter a mob.

—Unnamed Elvis fan, Internet chat room

On August 16, 1977, Elvis was found dead in his bathroom at Graceland. He was forty-two years old. The official cause of death was listed as cardiac arrhythmia, but there were also vast quantities of prescription drugs found in his body.

In the years following Elvis's death, tens of thousands of grieving fans flooded Memphis during the third week of August to honor his memory. August 16 soon came to be known as "Death Day" and the week that precedes it as "Elvis Week."

The highlight of the week is the candlelight vigil. Fans lining the street in front of Graceland are given candles lit from the eternal flame in the Meditation Garden, where Elvis is buried. They reverently file past his grave and often leave flowers, teddy bears, or other gifts to show their adoration.

E Is for Ed Sullivan

I want to say to Elvis Presley and the country that
this is a real decent, fine boy.

—Ed Sullivan

Elvis appeared on several different television shows in the mid-1950s, including Jimmy and Tommy Dorsey's *Stage Show*, *The Milton Berle Show*, and *The Steve Allen Show*.

But it was his appearance on *The Ed Sullivan Show* in 1956 that made Elvis a superstar. Though Sullivan had once sworn that he would never allow Elvis on his show, he changed his mind once he realized how many advertising dollars Elvis could generate. But he insisted that Elvis be filmed from the waist up so that viewers wouldn't be offended by the singer's swiveling hips.

Sullivan paid Elvis $50,000 for three television appearances, far more than he had ever paid any other performer. More than 50 million viewers watched those three shows.

F Is for Friends

It was something about Elvis's innocence we were all trying to protect.

—Billy Smith, Elvis's cousin

Growing up, Elvis was a loner with few close friends. After he became rich and famous, he surrounded himself with a group of men whom he affectionately called "the Guys." Some of them were relatives, some were employees, and some were simply hangers-on.

The press had another name for Elvis's friends. Because they often dressed in sunglasses and identical black mohair suits, reporters began calling the entourage "the Memphis Mafia." The name stuck, and the guys never objected. In fact, most of them found the term amusing.

The dozen or so men who were at various times a part of the Memphis Mafia formed a tight-knit brotherhood with only one purpose—to do Elvis's bidding and to protect his name and image.

G Is for Graceland

I think I'm going to like this new home. We will have a lot more
privacy and a lot more room to put some of the things we
have accumulated over the past few years.

—Gladys Presley

In 1957, Elvis paid $100,000 for a mansion built in the 1930s by a Memphis doctor. It was named Graceland in honor of the builder's Aunt Grace.

Elvis decorated Graceland's eighteen rooms in lavish style. The grounds of his mansion eventually included a swimming pool, riding stable, racquetball court, shooting gallery, and a coop for his mother's chickens. The property is fronted by a limestone wall and is entered through gates featuring musical notes and two guitar-playing Elvises.

In 1982, five years after Elvis died, Graceland was opened as a tourist attraction. More than 700,000 visitors tour Elvis's home each year, making it the second-most-visited house in the United States. Only the White House is more popular.

H Is for "Hound Dog"

I did The Steve Allen Show, *and they wnted to tame me down, so they had me dressed in a tuxedo and singing to a dog on a stool.*

—Elvis Presley

Elvis began including "Hound Dog," a song first made a hit by rhythm-and-blues artist Big Mama Thornton, in his live performances in early 1956. It quickly became one of his favorites.

He was delighted when entertainer Steve Allen asked him to perform the song on his television show. But when he learned that Allen wanted him to dress in formalwear and sing to a live basset hound costumed in collar, bowtie, and top hat, his enthusiasm waned. Elvis—and the dog—did the show anyway.

Elvis's recorded single "Hound Dog" was released in July 1956 and went gold just a few days later. He soon began opening or closing all his performances with the song, which remains one of his most popular recordings of all time.

I Is for Impersonators

If life was fair, Elvis would be alive and the impersonators would be dead.

—Johnny Carson

Thousands of entertainers of both sexes and many shapes, sizes, and nationalities impersonate Elvis. They dress like him and perform his songs at parties, reunions, conventions, county fairs, and weddings.

Elvis wigs, masks, clothing, and accessories are among the most popular items at costume rental companies throughout the world. Elvis impersonators range from professionals who look, sound, and move like the real Elvis to amateurs who perform more for fun than money.

Why do people pay money to watch an impersonator pretend to be Elvis? Maybe it's to relive the magic they once experienced hearing and seeing Elvis himself sing.

J Is for Jeweled Jumpsuits

President Richard Nixon: *You dress kind of strange, don't you?*

Elvis: *Well, Mr. President, you have your show and I have mine.*

Elvis of the 1970s looked very different from the rock-and-roll rebel Elvis of the 1950s. Gone were the pink-and-black outfits, the greasy ducktail, and the blue suede shoes.

Elvis's favorite costumes in his later career were jumpsuits—one-piece outfits with high collars and bell-bottom pants. Most of his jumpsuits were studded with rhinestones and sequins and were worn with a wide belt set with real rubies. Every jumpsuit had a matching cape, lined with gold fabric and modeled after Elvis's boyhood comic book hero Captain Marvel.

Some of Elvis's costumes were so elaborate that they weighed more than thirty pounds!

K Is for King of Rock and Roll

Elvis is the deity supreme of rock-and-roll religion
as it exists in today's form.
—Bob Dylan

When Elvis burst onto the music scene in the 1950s, his unique way of combining traditional country music with the rhythm and blues of the black community took the country by storm.

Sun Records owner Sam Phillips had once said that if he could find a white man who could sing like a black man, he could make a million dollars. Elvis was that man. The gritty rhythmic beat of his music and the lyrics that focused on rebellion and young love demanded a whole new label—rock and roll.

For the first time ever, teenagers had a category of music all their own. They crowned the man who introduced it to them "the King." And the King he remains, decades after his death.

 Is for *Love Me Tender*

A Presley picture is the only sure thing in show business.

—Hal Wallis, producer

Elvis enjoyed being a singing star. He enjoyed most of the television appearances he made. But more than anything else, he dreamed of becoming a famous movie actor.

In 1956, Elvis starred in *Love Me Tender*, a low-budget movie about the Civil War. Although most critics made fun of the movie, Elvis fans loved it.

Elvis went on to star in more than thirty movies. He was often romantically linked with his costars, especially actress Ann-Margret. Elvis's last movie, *Change of Habit,* was made in 1969.

Although Elvis never lost the ambition to be a serious actor, most of his films were considered nothing but fluff. But Elvis fans went to see them anyway, by the millions. Elvis never made a movie that lost money.

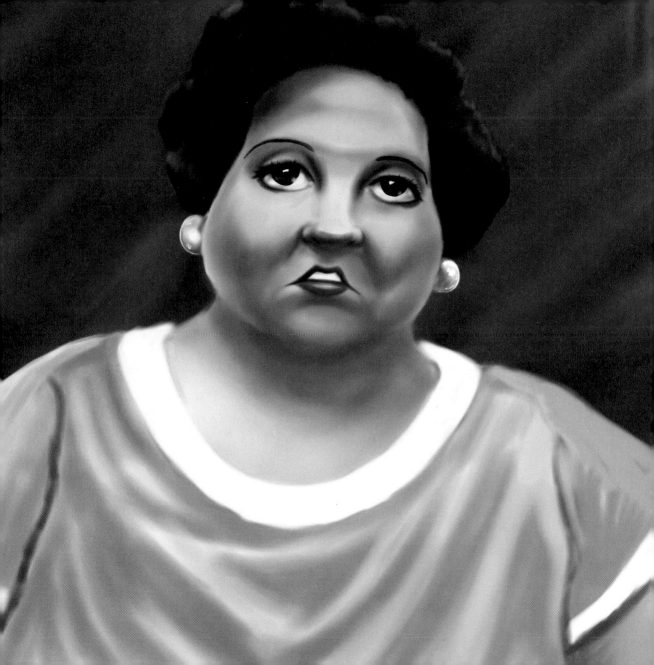

M Is for Mama

Mama was always my best girl.
—Elvis Presley

Early on the cold winter morning of January 8, 1935, a young man named Vernon Presley paced the floor while his wife, Gladys, gave birth to twin boys—Elvis Aron and his brother, Jesse Garon. Jesse was born dead.

Perhaps because of Jesse's death, Gladys was very protective of her only living child. She walked Elvis to school every day until he was a teenager. She refused to buy him a bicycle for his eleventh birthday, fearing he'd fall and hurt himself. She bought him a guitar instead.

Gladys and Vernon never lived apart from Elvis except when Elvis was in basic training with the army. It was during that time that Gladys became gravely ill. Elvis barely made it home in time to tell her good-bye. Her death, on August 14, 1958, completely devastated him.

N Is for Nobody

I don't sound like nobody.
—Elvis Presley

Eighteen-year-old Elvis walked into Sun Recording Studio in Memphis in the summer of 1953 to make a record to give his mother. But in his heart, he was hoping something bigger would happen once the folks at Sun heard him sing.

Marion Keisker helped Sun owner Sam Phillips run the business. "What do you sing?" she asked Elvis. He hesitated. There weren't many kinds of music he didn't know or like.

"I sing all kinds," he told her.

"Who do you sound like?"

"I don't sound like nobody," Elvis replied.

The rest is history. Within two years, Elvis Presley—who really didn't sound like "nobody"—was the biggest singing sensation in the country.

O Is for Overweight

He's not just a little out of shape, not just a little chubbier
than usual. The Living Legend is fat.

—The Hollywood Reporter, February 6, 1973

Elvis loved to eat. Perhaps his fondness for food went back to his childhood when sometimes there wasn't enough supper on the table. The foods he craved were high in fat, sugar, and calories. His favorite meal was peanut butter, bacon, and banana sandwiches, fried until they were golden brown.

By the time he was forty years old, Elvis weighed almost 250 pounds. His face was swollen and pasty and his eyes were puffy. Even his high-collared jumpsuits couldn't hide his double chin.

The diet pills Elvis took didn't slim him down, but they did make him nervous and jumpy. So he took tranquilizers to calm himself—a dangerous combination that may have cost him his life.

P Is for Priscilla

Once you got a taste of Elvis's universe, you never wanted to leave it.
—Priscilla Presley

Elvis met Priscilla Beaulieu in 1958 while he was stationed with the U.S. Army in Germany. He was twenty-three years old; she was fourteen. After his discharge, Elvis persuaded Priscilla's parents to allow her to move to Memphis to finish high school. Elvis's father and stepmother were to serve as the couple's chaperones.

Priscilla and Elvis were married in a secret ceremony in Las Vegas on May 1, 1967. Exactly nine months later, their daughter Lisa Marie was born.

The troubled marriage ended in divorce in 1973. But the couple remained friends to each other and devoted parents to their only child, who has followed in her father's footsteps to become a celebrity herself.

Is for Quartet

A lot of times the band and I will go up to our suite and sing until
daylight—gospel songs. We grew up with it. Gospel more or less
puts your mind at ease. It does mine.

—Elvis Presley

The gospel music Elvis loved was often performed by a quartet—four people singing
in harmony. His favorite quartets were the Blackwood Brothers and the Statesmen.

At a young age, Elvis began imitating the techniques of gospel quartets. He
admired the emotional way they sang their spirituals—with heads thrown back, feet
stomping, and hands extended toward the audience. Elvis used many of those same
movements in his performances.

Several different quartets sang backup for Elvis during his career. Some of the
most famous were the Jordanaires, the Imperials, the Sweet Inspirations (a female
group), and J. D. Sumner and the Stamps Quartet.

R Is for Rich

*Don't you worry none, Mama. When I grow up, I'm gonna buy you a fine
house and pay everything you owe at the grocery store and get two
Cadillacs—one for you and Daddy and one for me.*
—Elvis Presley

Elvis was born during the Great Depression of the 1930s. Many people were poor,
but the Presleys were among the poorest of all. They often had to rely on the charity of
friends and relatives just to survive.

All that changed when Elvis became a superstar. He bought dozens of cars and
motorcycles and even a $2 million jet airplane. He spent untold amounts of money
redecorating Graceland. He had so many diamonds that he hired a personal jeweler to
travel with him. And he gave elaborate gifts to family, friends, and even perfect strangers.

Over the course of his lifetime, Elvis earned, spent, and gave away several million
dollars. In 1966, he was the largest single taxpayer in the United States and the
highest paid entertainer on earth.

S Is for Sightings

ELVIS IS ALIVE! Exclusive Interview—First Since Aug. 16, 1977

—Weekly World News, September 6, 2004

When Elvis died on August 16, 1977, some of his fans refused to accept that the King was really gone. Rumors began to spread that Elvis wasn't dead at all—he had only gone into hiding to get some rest.

Supermarket tabloids frequently published stories of people who claimed to have sighted Elvis at convenience stores, amusement parks, and fast-food restaurants. Other stories claimed that Elvis was abducted by aliens and taken to live on another planet.

Many fans believe that Elvis's spirit still lingers on earth and that he sends messages from the grave. Photographers have even shot pictures of clouds shaped exactly like Elvis's profile in the sky over Graceland.

T Is for Tupelo

The most significant landmark of Tupelo's modern history is a modest, two-room house where the King of Rock and Roll was born on January 8, 1935.
—Tupelo Visitors Bureau

The shotgun shack where Elvis was born is part of the fifteen-acre Elvis Presley Park in Tupelo, a town of 25,000 people in northeast Mississippi. The park also contains a chapel, museum, gift shop, picnic area, and a life-sized bronze statue of Elvis as a young teenager.

A driving tour through Tupelo includes the elementary and junior high schools Elvis attended, the Assembly of God church where his family worshiped, Johnnie's Drive-In (where Elvis enjoyed cheeseburgers and onion rings), and the Tupelo Hardware Store (where his mother bought his first guitar).

Elvis lived in Tupelo until his family moved to Memphis, Tennessee, when he was thirteen years old.

U Is for U.S. Army

We can't have Elvis pull any favors. The country doesn't look favorably on
boys who shirk their duty to the military.

—Colonel Tom Parker

Elvis received an army draft notice in December, 1957. He could have requested assignment to the entertainment corps of the Special Services, but he instead chose to be a regular GI. His primary assignment was to drive a jeep.

Elvis was shipped overseas to Bremerhaven, Germany. Though he spent his days much like any other soldier, his nights were spent signing autographs for adoring German fans and reading hundreds of letters from fans in the United States.

Elvis was discharged from the army in 1960. He returned home and picked up right where he had left off—starring in *G.I. Blues*, a movie based on his military experience.

V Is for Vegas

By the time Elvis was doing Vegas in the early seventies, his voice had strengthened, his range had widened, his soul had deepened. He saw he still had something he thought he'd lost—the ability to move a live audience to tears.

—Priscilla Presley

Elvis bombed when he appeared in Las Vegas for the first time in 1956. The conservative, middle-aged audience didn't care for his raucous style of entertainment.

By the 1960s that attitude had changed. The Elvis movie *Viva Las Vegas* was a hit in that city and everywhere else in the country. By the end of the decade, Elvis was making regular appearances in Las Vegas and quickly became the most popular and highly paid act to ever perform there.

Today the memory of Elvis is kept alive in Las Vegas by countless impersonators, souvenir shops, museums, wedding chapels, and stage shows.

W Is for Women

*If I slept with every woman the weekly magazines
say I have, I would have been dead a long time ago.*
—Elvis Presley

Elvis loved women. And women loved Elvis. From first girlfriend Dixie Locke to final girlfriend Ginger Alden, Elvis was surrounded by adoring females his entire adult life.

Rioting hordes of teenage girls screamed at the top of their lungs through Elvis's live performances in the 1950s. Millions of female fans lined up outside theaters in the 1960s to buy tickets to his movies. And in the 1970s, women fought each other for the sweat-soaked scarves Elvis threw into the audience during his Las Vegas stage shows.

What was it about Elvis that women loved? His looks? His voice? His money? His Southern-gentleman manners? Most likely it was a combination of all those things. But one thing is for sure—even in death, women the world over still adore Elvis.

# X Is for X-Rated

I don't mean anything dirty by the way I move. When I sing rock and roll,
my legs just won't stand still. I don't care what they say, it ain't nasty.

—Elvis Presley

When Elvis burst onto the music scene in the 1950s, there was no such term as "X-rated." But many adults used the words "lewd," "obscene," and "vulgar" to describe the way Elvis moved when he sang.

Elvis used his whole body when he performed. He swiveled his hips. He jiggled his legs. He curled his lips and threw back his head. His gyrations soon earned him the nickname "Elvis the Pelvis."

Teenagers went wild over this sexy new style of performing. They finally had their own hero and their own kind of music. And many of them didn't care whether their parents liked it or not.

Y Is for "Young Elvis"

The Elvis stamp is the top-selling commemorative
postage stamp of all time.
—United States Postal Service

In 1992, the U.S. Postal Service decided to issue a stamp in memory of Elvis. They let the American public vote on whether to picture the young rock-and-roll Elvis of the 1950s or the jumpsuit-clad older Elvis of the 1970s.

"Young Elvis" won by a landslide. The postal service released the twenty-nine-cent stamp in ceremonies at Graceland on the day that would have been Elvis's fifty-eighth birthday.

Stamp collectors around the world were thrilled. They bought more than 500 million Elvis stamps, three times the number usually printed by the postal service.

Z Is for Zillions

Zillion: an indeterminately large number.

—Merriam-Webster's Collegiate Dictionary

If there really were such a number as "zillions," it could be used in relation to Elvis.

His records have sold more than one billion copies around the world. He earned 84 Gold Records, 45 Platinum Records, and 21 Multi-Platinum Records.

Millions of fans have watched the thirty-one movies in which Elvis starred. His television and live performances set viewing and attendance records that have never been matched. More than 15 million people have visited Graceland and hundreds of thousands have toured Elvis's birthplace in Tupelo.

What number do you get when you multiply thousands by millions by billions? Zillions!

Reflections on the King

Elvis Presley can't last. I tell you flatly, he can't last.

—Jackie Gleason

Elvis Presley is the greatest cultural force of the twentieth century.

—Leonard Bernstein

I wouldn't let my daughter walk across the street to see Elvis Presley.

—Billy Graham

Elvis Presley taught white Americans to get down.

—James Brown

Elvis Presley's death deprives our country of a part of itself.

—Jimmy Carter

I love Elvis Presley's music because he was my generation.
But then again, Elvis is everyone's generation.

—Margaret Thatcher

Elvis in Film

1956	*Love Me Tender*	Twentieth Century Fox
1957	*Loving You*	Paramount
1957	*Jailhouse Rock*	Metro-Goldwyn-Mayer
1958	*King Creole*	Paramount
1960	*G.I. Blues*	Paramount
1960	*Flaming Star*	Twentieth Century Fox
1961	*Wild in the Country*	Twentieth Century Fox
1961	*Blue Hawaii*	Paramount
1962	*Follow That Dream*	United Artists
1962	*Kid Galahad*	United Artists
1962	*Girls! Girls! Girls!*	Paramount
1963	*It Happened at the World's Fair*	Metro-Goldwyn-Mayer
1963	*Fun in Acapulco*	Paramount
1964	*Kissin' Cousins*	Metro-Goldwyn-Mayer
1964	*Viva Las Vegas*	Metro-Goldwyn-Mayer
1964	*Roustabout*	Paramount
1965	*Girl Happy*	Metro-Goldwyn-Mayer
1965	*Tickle Me*	Allied Artists
1965	*Harum Scarum*	Metro-Goldwyn-Mayer
1966	*Frankie and Johnny*	United Artists
1966	*Paradise, Hawaiian Style*	Paramount
1966	*Spinout*	Metro-Goldwyn-Mayer
1967	*Easy Come, Easy Go*	Paramount
1967	*Double Trouble*	Metro-Goldwyn-Mayer
1967	*Clambake*	United Artists
1968	*Stay Away, Joe*	Metro-Goldwyn-Mayer
1968	*Speedway*	Metro-Goldwyn-Mayer
1968	*Live a Little, Love a Little*	Metro-Goldwyn-Mayer
1969	*Charro!*	National General
1969	*The Trouble with Girls*	Metro-Goldwyn-Mayer
1969	*Change of Habit*	Universal

Elvis Goes Platinum

Nine Times Platinum

Elvis' Christmas Album (1970 package)

Six Times Platinum

Elvis' Gold Records, vol. 1

Five Times Platinum

Aloha from Hawaii

Four Times Platinum

The Top Ten Hits

Three Times Platinum

Blue Hawaii

Elvis 30 #1 Hits

*Elvis as Recorded at Madison
Square Garden*

*Elvis Sings the Wonderful World
of Christmas*

Elvis' Christmas Album (1957 package)

The Number One Hits

You'll Never Walk Alone

Two Times Platinum

50 Years–50 Hits

Amazing Grace

*Elvis, A Legendary Performer,
vols. 1 & 2*

Elvis in Concert

*Elvis, The King of Rock 'n' Roll, The
Complete 50's Masters*

*Elvis Sings Burning Love and Hits from
His Movies, vol. 2*

How Great Thou Art

Moody Blue

Pure Gold

The Elvis Presley Story

50 Worldwide Gold Award Hits

Platinum

50,000,000 Elvis Fans Can't Be Wrong
(Elvis' Gold Records, vol. 2)

Almost in Love

Double Dynamite

Elvis 2nd to None

Elvis Aron Presley

Elvis, From Nashville to Memphis,
The Essential 60's Masters I

Elvis, His Greatest Hits
(Reader's Digest compilation)

NBC-TV Special

Flaming Star

Elvis Sings Hits from His Movies, vol. 1

Elvis' Gold Records, vol. 3

Frankie and Johnny

G.I. Blues

He Touched Me

His Hand in Mine

If Every Day Was Like Christmas

It's Christmas Time

Let's Be Friends

On Stage, February 1970

Separate Ways

Welcome to My World

Worldwide Gold Award Hits, vols. 1 & 2
(club version)

My Elvis

I was born in 1954, the year Elvis cut his first record. I don't remember the rock-and-roll rebel Elvis of the 1950s. My Elvis was the Hollywood star of the 1960s who made one fun-but-forgettable movie after another and who seemed in danger of becoming little more than a caricature as British rock groups like the Beatles and the Rolling Stones took America and the world by storm.

Then came 1969, with "Cold Kentucky Rain," "In the Ghetto," and "Suspicious Minds." Elvis was back, and better than ever. But I'd known that when he starred in his *Comeback Special* on television a year earlier. I'll wager that female fans of all ages went just as crazy as the teeny-boppers of the 1950s had when Elvis—toned, tanned, and dressed in black leather—took the stage in 1968. I know I did.

As a matter of fact, more than a quarter century after his death, I still do.

—Jennie Ivey

My Elvis

Elvis Presley was born in 1935, three years before my birth. We were both natives of the early twentieth-century South; Elvis of Mississippi and Memphis and I of northeast Texas. Both of us were subject to the influence of the biracial South. Elvis integrated himself into African-American culture more than I did.

When Elvis recorded "That's All Right" in 1954, I was a junior in high school. Elvis performed many times on the *Louisiana Hayride* in Shreveport and toured areas of east Texas near my home, but I never saw him in person. I didn't even know anyone who had.

All the girls I knew were just wild about Elvis. Teenagers would gather in someone's home and play Elvis music on 45 RPM singles. While we listened to his songs, the boys wanted to dance, but the girls were so excited by Elvis's voice that they could think of nothing else. I harbored a jealousy of the girls' attention to Elvis, and of the corresponding lack of attention toward me. As a result, I was not an Elvis fan. I preferred the popular quartets of the time—the Hilltoppers, the Four Freshmen, and others.

After Elvis died, I became a fan. By that time I was aware of the great musical talent of the King, and of the influence that he exerted on the second half of the twentieth century. Besides, Elvis's music was so much better than much of what followed him. As a history professor I always delivered an enthusiastic lecture in my Tennessee history classes about Elvis, emphasizing his importance to our state and to the history of music.

—W. Calvin Dickinson

My Elvis

My most lasting memory of Elvis happened when I was eleven years old. I had never thought much about him except to know that my parents, aunts, and uncles would stop everything to hear an Elvis song on the radio, watch an Elvis movie on our black-and-white TV set, or even see him on stage in person. But all that changed on August 16, 1977.

My dad, who was known for his practical jokes, walked through the kitchen door at suppertime and announced, "Elvis is dead!"

"Gene, don't say that," my mother scolded as she continued cooking.

"It's true," Dad told my aunts, uncles, and cousins, who were all visiting. "It really is true."

No one believed him. "What's the punch line?" my uncle asked. Sad to say, there was no punch line. My dad turned on the radio and we heard Elvis singing. At the end of the song, the local deejay announced that the King had died today. Our kitchen went silent and tears filled everyone's eyes. At the time, I just couldn't understand why adults were so broken up over the death of a man they had never personally met.

Today, I understand and appreciate who Elvis was. I understand how he was able to touch and affect so many people in a very real and personal way. The King is not dead. He continues to live in the hearts of his adoring fans.

—Lisa W. Rand

My Elvis

Elvis was a legend long before I had ever heard of him. He was gone four years before I was born. My first memory of Elvis was seeing him in an advertisement for an oldies CD. Not everyone knows the details of Elvis's life, but everyone eventually knows that he was and always will be the King of Rock and Roll.

    Only recently have I had the chance to know Elvis as more than a legend. Through the research and effort I have put into illustrating this book—trying to capture the essence of Elvis—I have grown to know and to love Elvis just as much as millions of other fans know and love him.

—Ron Wireman Jr.

Jennie Ivey is a former history teacher who lives in Cookeville, Tennessee, with her husband, George, and their three children. She works as a columnist for the *Herald-Citizen* newspaper and writes fiction and nonfiction for various other publications.

W. Calvin Dickinson is a professor emeritus at Tennessee Technological University, where he taught history for thirty years before retiring in 2000. He is the author of fifteen books. He and his wife, Charlene, live in Cookeville, Tennessee.

Lisa W. Rand teaches elementary school and is an adjunct instructor in the College of Education at Tennessee Technological University. She lives in Cookeville, Tennessee, with her husband, Richard, and daughter, Victoria.

Ivey, Dickinson, and Rand are coauthors of *Tennessee Tales the Textbooks Don't Tell*, published in 2002 by Overmountain Press.

Illustrator **Ron Wireman Jr.** graduated from the Columbus College of Art and Design in 2003. He is currently enrolled at Tennessee Technological University studying Art Education. Ron has worked as a professional artist since 2001, painting caricatures, murals, and portraits.